Searchlight
BOOKS™

Space Mysteries

T0373977

Mysteries of
Mars

Rebecca E. Hirsch

Lerner Publications ◆ Minneapolis

Lerner Publications Company
An imprint of Lerner Publishing Group, Inc.
241 First Avenue North
Minneapolis, MN 55401 USA

For reading levels and more information, look up this title at www.lernerbooks.com.

Main body text set in Adrianna Regular.
Typeface provided by Chank.

Designer: Mary Ross

Library of Congress Cataloging-in-Publication Data

Names: Hirsch, Rebecca E., author.
Title: Mysteries of Mars / Rebecca E. Hirsch.
Other titles: Searchlight books. Space mysteries.
Description: Minneapolis : Lerner Publications, [2021] I Series: Searchlight books. Space
    mysteries I Includes bibliographical references and index. I Audience: Ages 8–11 I
    Audience: Grades 4–6 I Summary: "Could there be life on Mars? Scientists are trying
    to answer this and many other mysteries about our next-door planetary neighbor.
    This exciting title introduces young readers to the current scientific mysteries
    surrounding Mars."— Provided by publisher.
Identifiers: LCCN 2019045826 (print) I LCCN 2019045827 (ebook) I
    ISBN 9781541597365 (library binding) I ISBN 9781728413877 (paperback) I
    ISBN 9781728400884 (ebook)
Subjects: LCSH: Mars (Planet)—Juvenile literature. I Mars (Planet)—Exploration—
    Juvenile literature.
Classification: LCC QB641 .H57 2021 (print) I LCC QB641 (ebook) I DDC 523.43—dc23

LC record available at https://lccn.loc.gov/2019045826
LC ebook record available at https://lccn.loc.gov/2019045827

Manufactured in the United States of America
1-47840-48280-1/23/2020

Contents

Chapter 1

EXPLORING MARS . . . 4

Chapter 2

WET OR DRY? . . . 8

Chapter 3

THE SEARCH FOR LIFE . . . 14

Chapter 4

MISSION TO MARS . . . 22

3D Printer Activity • 29
Glossary • 30
Learn More about Mars • 31
Index • 32

EXPLORING MARS

Mars is a cold, alien world. It is the fourth planet from the sun and our nearest neighbor in the solar system.

Mars is about half the size of Earth. It has less gravity than Earth. If you weighed 100 pounds (45 kg) on Earth, you would weigh just 38 pounds (17 kg) on Mars.

Mars is named after the ancient Roman god of war.

Most of Mars's surface is covered with red rocks and dust.

Earth and Mars are very different worlds. Earth is warm and wet. About 71 percent of its surface is covered with oceans.

But Mars is a frozen desert. It has no rivers, lakes, or oceans. Icy dust swirls in the air. The average temperature is -80°F (-62°C).

The atmosphere on Mars is much thinner than the atmosphere on Earth. This thin atmosphere gives Mars less protection from dangerous rays of the sun.

Mysterious Mars

People have known about Mars since ancient times. If you look up at the sky on a clear night, you can see Mars without a telescope. It looks like a red star. Mars looks red because its surface is covered with rust. Many people call it the Red Planet.

Aside from Earth, Mars is the most explored planet in the solar system. We have sent spacecraft to orbit the planet. We have landed rovers that drive around the surface, taking pictures and measurements. Yet the planet remains full of mystery.

One mystery is why the northern half of Mars looks so different from the southern half. The northern half of the planet is flat and smooth. The southern half is rough and covered with craters.

What makes the two halves so different? Scientists have an idea. The north half could be so smooth because it was once covered by an ocean.

But Mars has no ocean. It is a dry, dusty planet. Was Mars different long ago? If it had an ocean, maybe Mars was once more like Earth.

Winds and temperature changes cause Martian sand dunes to move and change shape.

Chapter 2

WET OR DRY?

In 1976, two US spacecraft, *Viking 1* and *Viking 2*, traveled to Mars. The spacecraft sent landers to the surface. The *Viking* spacecraft took the first close-up photographs of the surface of Mars.

Each of the *Viking* landers was about 10 feet (3 m) across and 7 feet (2 m) tall.

Viking 1 took the first image ever from Mars's surface.

The pictures showed some mysterious features. No signs of liquid water were on the surface of Mars, but there were features that looked like dry riverbeds. These features looked similar to riverbeds on Earth.

Liquid water can't last on the surface of present-day Mars. The atmosphere is too thin. Any water would quickly boil away. But the riverbeds suggest that Mars was different long ago.

Since *Viking 1* and *Viking 2*, other spacecraft have explored the Red Planet. The twin rovers, *Spirit* and *Opportunity*, landed in 2004. They took photos of the Martian surface. Both rovers found signs of past water.

Opportunity found another clue. The rover studied rocks on the ground near its landing site. It discovered minerals that form in water inside the rocks. This showed the rocks had once been wet. It looked like *Opportunity*'s landing site had once been the shore of a salty sea.

NASA's *Opportunity* rover explored Mars for fourteen years before it fell silent after a dust storm in 2018.

STEM Spotlight

Since 2012, NASA's *Curiosity* rover has been exploring the Gale Crater. This crater has a mountain in the middle made of layers of rock. Each layer is from a different time. By testing the layers, *Curiosity* can tell scientists about the history of Mars. *Curiosity* drills into the rock to make rock powder. It drops the powder into another instrument to study the minerals. *Curiosity* has discovered that Gale Crater once had water.

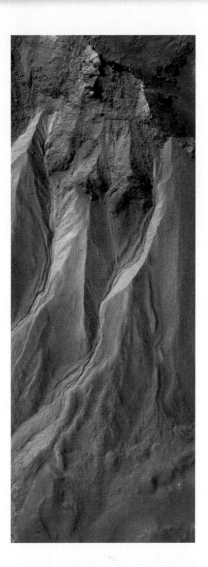

Scientists are unsure what causes these strange dark streaks to appear on Mars's mountains.

Water World

Present-day Mars does have ice at its poles, but it has no standing water. But could liquid water still flow on Mars?

Spacecraft have spotted dark streaks on Martian hillsides. The streaks look similar to ones on Earth formed by salt water. Maybe salt water is running down the hillsides.

A spacecraft that orbits Mars snapped pictures of the streaks. When scientists studied the pictures, they found streaks only on the steepest slopes. This could mean that the streaks aren't a sign of water. They could be sand sliding downhill. The answer remains a mystery.

Other signs of liquid water have been found on Mars. A spacecraft used radar to discover a big lake deep under the Martian surface.

Any sign of liquid water on Mars is exciting. Almost everywhere that there is water on Earth, there is life. On Earth, living things even survive in lakes deep under the ground.

Could the same thing be true on Mars? Scientists have yet to find out.

THE KOROLEV CRATER NEAR MARS'S NORTH POLE IS FILLED WITH FROZEN WATER.

▼

Chapter 3

THE SEARCH FOR LIFE

Mars doesn't seem like a promising place for life. But ancient Mars was different. Could life have been there in the past? And could it still be there?

This stripe across Mars's surface is a huge canyon called Valles Marineris. It is one of the largest canyons in the solar system.

Space fact or fiction?

In 1996, NASA scientists found fossils, or traces of living things, inside a Martian rock, meaning Mars once had life!

That turned out to be fiction. When scientists made their big announcement, they thought they had found fossils. But when other scientists studied the rock, they weren't convinced. They think the "fossils" were far too small to be actual microbes. Most scientists no longer believe the rock contains evidence of life from Mars. The search for Martian life continues.

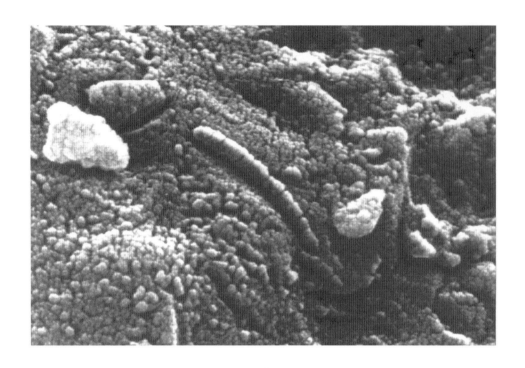

SCIENTISTS THOUGHT THESE TINY
TUBES FOUND IN A MARTIAN
METEORITE MIGHT BE FOSSILS.

Scientists think any life on Mars would be minuscule microbes. Microbes are so small that they can be seen only with a microscope.

Even if microbes once existed on Mars, they may have become extinct. But if they did exist, they would have left signs behind.

Signs of Life

Rovers are searching for signs of past life. They are looking at Martian rocks to try to find fossils. Finding fossils might tell us that life once existed on Mars.

NASA's *Curiosity* rover tests the soil on Mars for signs of life.

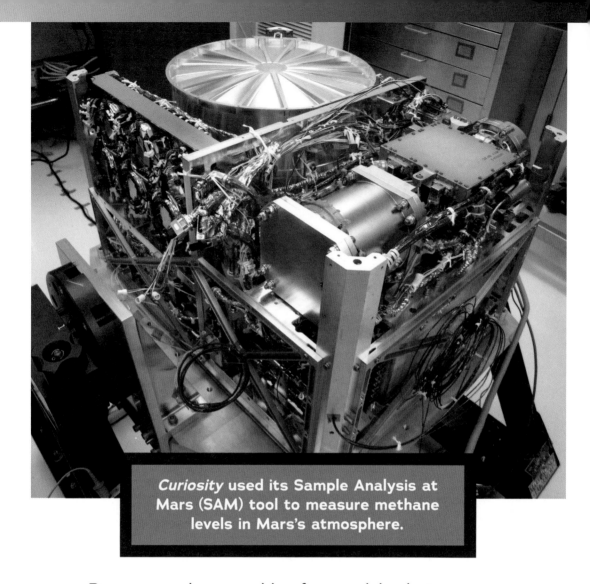

Curiosity used its Sample Analysis at Mars (SAM) tool to measure methane levels in Mars's atmosphere.

Rovers are also searching for special substances that living things leave behind. These substances can be another sign of life. One key substance is a gas called methane. Telescopes and spacecraft have found methane in the Martian atmosphere. On Earth almost all methane is made by living things. What is making the methane on Mars?

The *Curiosity* rover, which landed in 2012, uncovered a clue. It discovered that the amount of methane rises in summer and falls in winter. Whatever is making the methane changes throughout the year.

One possibility is that microbes are making the methane. That would mean Mars has microbes living on it! The microbes might survive underground, rather than on the surface.

The red spots on this map show where scientists found large amounts of methane during the summer.

But the methane might be from an underground lake, instead of from living things. The methane could seep out through the ground. Perhaps more methane seeps out in summer than in winter.

Is Mars's methane a sign of life? Scientists need more clues to answer this question.

THIS CHART SHOWS HOW THE AMOUNT OF METHANE IN MARS'S ATMOSPHERE RISES AND FALLS DURING THE SEASONS.

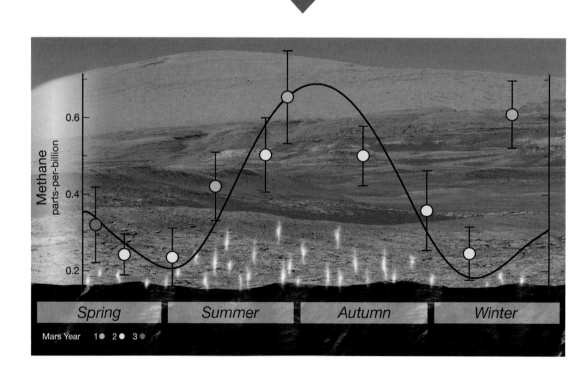

Methane parts-per-billion

0.6

0.4

0.2

| Spring | Summer | Autumn | Winter |

Mars Year 1 ● 2 ● 3 ●

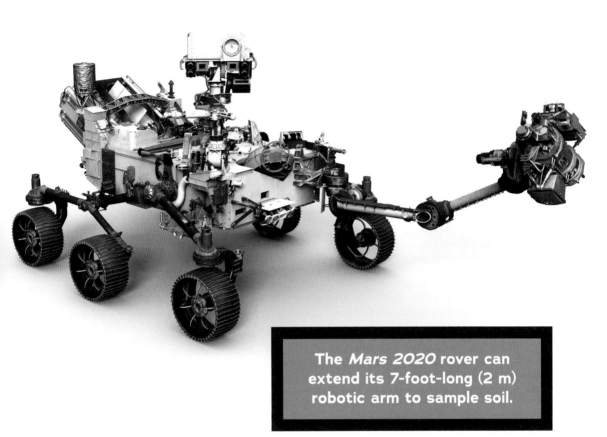

The *Mars 2020* rover can extend its 7-foot-long (2 m) robotic arm to sample soil.

Mars 2020 is a new rover that was sent to Mars in July 2020. It will continue to look for signs of life. It has a laser to look underground so it can make maps of the layers of rock, water, and ice just under the surface.

The new rover will also drill into rocks and collect samples of rocks and soil. It will store these samples in tubes. The tubes could ride back to Earth on a future mission. These samples could reveal Mars's biggest secrets.

Chapter 4

MISSION TO MARS

Mars has so many mysteries. How can we ever solve them all? To find answers, people might have to go there to investigate.

But Mars isn't at all friendly for humans. It has very thin air that people can't breathe, no liquid water on the surface, and very cold weather.

Astronauts on Mars would conduct science experiments.

IF HUMANS EVER WENT TO MARS, THEY WOULD HAVE TO WEAR SPACE SUITS TO BREATHE AND STAY WARM.

Mars also has little protection from the sun's harmful rays. On Earth, a magnetic field and a thick atmosphere protect the planet from these rays. But Mars doesn't have a magnetic field or a thick atmosphere. The amount of radiation on Mars makes it a very dangerous place for people.

Could people ever survive in such a harsh place?

Robots Blaze a Trail

Rovers are testing how people could survive on Mars. These robot explorers might help make Mars safer for astronauts. *Curiosity* has measured the harmful rays from the sun. This information could help scientists come up with ways to protect future astronauts.

NASA's *Curiosity* rover can also measure the gases in the atmosphere and the materials in the ground.

Clouds made of frozen water particles
float over Mars's volcanoes.

Although Mars doesn't have breathable air or drinkable water, it does have raw materials. One useful material is the ice that sits on the Martian surface. Maybe future explorers could melt some of the ice to make water for drinking.

Astronauts could also use this water to make fuel. Water can be split into two other materials, hydrogen and oxygen. Hydrogen can be burned as fuel. This fuel could help send a spaceship back to Earth.

Another useful material is Martian air. It contains carbon dioxide, which can be split into carbon and oxygen. It could be used to make oxygen for breathing. The *Mars 2020* rover will contain an instrument called MOXIE. MOXIE is the size of a car battery. It will test how to make oxygen on Mars.

Technicians install MOXIE, the gold box (*pictured below*), into the *Mars 2020* rover.

STEM Spotlight

NASA is sending a helicopter drone (*below*) to Mars. Its body is about the size of a softball. Its blades are 4 feet (1.2 m) long. It will travel to Mars along with *Mars 2020*.

This helicopter could take pictures of places rovers can't go. It could soar over cliffs or the walls of craters. Someday, helicopters could even work alongside human explorers.

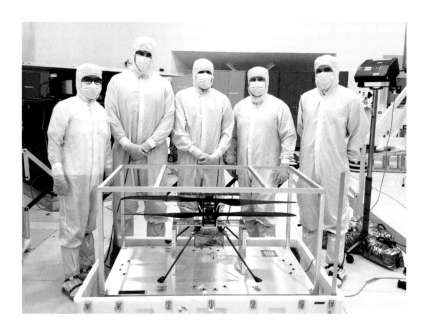

The Mars Helicopter can assist both rovers and human explorers.

Robot explorers will help test these new technologies. Maybe they will find ways that humans can survive on this harsh alien planet. And maybe the people who work and live there will finally solve the mysteries of Mars.

3D Printer Activity

NASA's *Curiosity* is roughly the size of a car, but you can use a 3D printer to create your own tiny version of the rover. Follow the below link to download the 3D printer file:

PAGE PLUS

https://qrs.lernerbooks.com/Curiosity

Glossary

atmosphere: the mixture of gases that surrounds a planet

carbon dioxide: an invisible, colorless gas that forms part of the atmosphere on Mars

crater: a hole in the ground created by something falling, such as a large chunk of rock

extinct: no longer living

fossil: a trace or the remains of a living thing from millions of years ago, preserved in rock

gravity: the force that pulls things toward a planet and keeps them from floating away

magnetic field: an invisible area around Earth that shields the planet from harmful radiation

methane: a colorless, odorless gas that is produced by living things

microscope: an instrument that makes very small objects appear larger so they can be seen

orbit: to travel in a circular path around something, such as a planet

rover: a wheeled robot that explores the surface of a moon or planet

telescope: an instrument that makes distant objects, such as planets, appear larger and closer

Learn More about Mars

Books

Carney, Elizabeth. *Mars: The Red Planet*. Washington, DC: National Geographic Kids, 2016. Check out this book to learn more about Earth's nearest neighbor.

Hirsch, Rebecca E. *Planets in Action (An Augmented Reality Experience)*. Minneapolis: Lerner Publications, 2020. Explore the latest discoveries about Mars and all the planets in the solar system.

Motum, Markus. Curiosity: *The Story of a Mars Rover*. Somerville, MA: Candlewick, 2018. This book will guide you through *Curiosity*'s journey on Mars.

Websites

NASA: Mars for Kids
https://mars.nasa.gov/participate/funzone/
Find Mars-related games, art projects, fascinating facts, and more ways to explore.

NASA Space Place: Mars
https://spaceplace.nasa.gov/all-about-mars/en/
See photos and learn facts about the Red Planet.

National Geographic Kids: Mission to Mars
https://kids.nationalgeographic.com/explore/space/mission-to-mars/
Get fast facts and photos about Mars, our next-door neighbor in space.

Index

astronauts, 24–25

Curiosity, 11, 19, 24, 29

ice, 12, 21, 25

Mars 2020, 21, 26–27
methane, 18–20
microbes, 15–16, 19

Opportunity, 10

oxygen, 25–26

rocks, 10–11, 15, 17, 21
rovers, 6, 10–11, 17–19, 21, 24, 26–27, 29

spacecraft, 6, 8, 10, 12–13, 18

water, 9–13, 21–22, 25

Photo Acknowledgments

ESA/DLR/FU Berlin (CC BY-SA 3.0 IGO), pp. 4, 13; NASA/JPL/USGS, p. 5; Peter Alfred Hess/flickr (CC BY 2.0), p. 6; NASA/JPL-Caltech/University of Arizona, pp. 7, 8, 11, 12; Roel van der Hoorn/NASA, p. 9; NASA/JPL/Cornell University/Maas Digital, p. 10; NASA/JPL-Caltech, pp. 14, 20, 21, 26, 27, 28, 29; NASA, pp. 15, 16, 23; NASA/JPL-Caltech/MSSS, pp. 17, 24; NASA/GSFC, p. 18; Trent Schindler/NASA, p. 19; NASA/JSC/Pat Rawlings, SAIC, p. 22; NASA/JPL/MSSS, p. 25.

Cover: NASA/JPL-Caltech/MSSS.